Bowen

by Iain Gray

PUBLISHING
WRITING *to* REMEMBER

79 Main Street, Newtongrange,
Midlothian EH22 4NA
Tel: 0131 344 0414   Fax: 0845 075 6085
E-mail: info@lang-syne.co.uk
www.langsyneshop.co.uk

Design by Dorothy Meikle
Printed by Printwell Ltd
© Lang Syne Publishers Ltd 2019

All rights reserved. No part of this publication may be reproduced, stored or introduced into a retrieval system, or transmitted in any form or by any means (electronic, mechanical, photocopying, recording or otherwise) without the prior written permission of Lang Syne Publishers Ltd.

ISBN 978-1-85217-658-7

Bowen

MOTTO:
To be, rather than to seem.

CREST:
A falcon.

NAME variations include:
Bohan
Bowan
Bowane
Bowene
Bowne
Bowin

Chapter one:

Origins of Welsh surnames

by Iain Gray

If you don't know where you came from, you won't know where you're going **is a frequently quoted observation and one that has a particular resonance today when there has been a marked upsurge in interest in genealogy, with increasing numbers of people curious to trace their family roots.**

Main sources for genealogical research include census returns and official records of births, marriages and deaths – and the key to unlocking the detail they contain is obviously a family surname, one that has been 'inherited' and passed from generation to generation.

No matter our station in life, we all have a surname – but it was not until about the middle of the fourteenth century that the practice of being identified by a particular, or 'fixed', surname became commonly established throughout the British Isles.

Previous to this, it was normal for a person to be identified through the use of only a forename.

Wales, however, known in the Welsh language as *Cymru*, is uniquely different – with the use of what are known as patronymic names continuing well into the fifteenth century and, in remote rural areas, up until the early nineteenth century.

Patronymic names are ones where a son takes his father's forename, or Christian name, as his surname.

Examples of patronymic names throughout the British Isles include 'Johnson', indicating 'son of John', while specifically in Scotland 'son of' was denoted by the prefix Mc or Mac – with 'MacDonald', for example, meaning 'son of Donald.'

Early Welsh law, known as *Cyfraith Hywel*, *The Law of Hywel*, introduced by Hywel the Good, who ruled from Prestatyn to Pembroke between 915 AD and 950 AD, stipulated that a person's name should indicate their ancestry – the name in effect being a type of 'family tree.'

This required the prefixes *ap* or *ab* – derived from *mab*, meaning 'son of' being placed before the person's baptismal name.

In the case of females, the suffixes *verch* or *ferch*, sometimes shortened to *vch* or *vz* would be attached to their Christian name to indicate 'daughter of.'

In some cases, rather than being known for

example as *Llewellyn ap Thomas* – *Llewellyn son of Thomas* – Llewellyn's name would incorporate an 'ancestral tree' going back much earlier than his father.

One source gives the example of *Llewellyn ap Thomas ap Dafydd ap Evan ap Owen ap John* – meaning *Llewellyn son of Thomas son of Dafydd son of Evan son of Owen son of John*.

This leads to great confusion, to say the least, when trying to trace a person's ancestry back to a particular family – with many people having the forenames, for example, of Llewellyn, Thomas, Owen or John.

The first Act of Union between Wales and England that took place in 1536 during the reign of Henry VIII required that all Welsh names be registered in an Anglicised form – with *Hywel*, for example, becoming Howell, or Powell, and *Gruffydd* becoming Griffiths.

An early historical example of this concerns William ap John Thomas, standard bearer to Henry VIII, who became William Jones.

In many cases – as in Davies and Williams – an s was simply added to the original patronymic name, while in other cases the prefix *ap* or *ab* was contracted to *p* or *b* to prefix the name – as in *ab Evan* to form Bevan and *ap Richard* to form Pritchard.

Other original Welsh surnames – such as Morgan, originally *Morcant* – derive from ancient Celtic sources, while others stem from a person's physical characteristics – as in *Gwyn* or *Wynne* a nickname for someone with fair hair, *Gough* or *Gooch* denoting someone with red hair or a ruddy complexion, *Gethin* indicating swarthy or ugly and *Lloyd* someone with brown or grey hair.

With many popular surnames found today in Wales being based on popular Christian names such as John, this means that what is known as the 'stock' or 'pool' of names is comparatively small compared to that of common surnames found in England, Scotland and Ireland.

This explains why, in a typical Welsh village or town with many bearers of a particular name not necessarily being related, they were differentiated by being known, for example, as 'Jones the butcher', 'Jones the teacher' and 'Jones the grocer.'

Another common practice, dating from about the nineteenth century, was to differentiate among families of the same name by prefixing it with the mother's surname or hyphenating the name.

The history of the origins and development of Welsh surnames is inextricably bound up with the nation's frequently turbulent history and its rich culture.

Speaking a Celtic language known as Brythonic, which would gradually evolve into Welsh, the natives were subjected to Roman invasion in 48 AD, and in the following centuries to invasion by the Anglo-Saxons, Vikings and Normans.

Under England's ruthless and ambitious Edward I, the nation was fortified with castles between 1276 and 1295 to keep the 'rebellious' natives in check – but this did not prevent a series of bloody uprisings against English rule that included, most notably, Owain Glyndŵr's rebellion in 1400.

Politically united with England through the first Act of Union in 1536, becoming part of the Kingdom of Great Britain in 1707 and part of the United Kingdom in 1801, it was in 1999 that *Cynulliad Cenedlaethol Cymru*, the National Assembly for Wales, was officially opened by the Queen.

Welsh language and literature has flourished throughout the nation's long history.

In what is known as the Heroic Age, early Welsh poets include the late sixth century Taliesin and Aneirin, author of *Y Gododdin*.

Discovered in a thirteenth century manuscript but thought to date from anywhere between the seventh and eleventh centuries, it refers to the kingdom of Gododdin that took in south-east Scotland and

Northumberland and was part of what was once the Welsh territory known as *Hen Ogledd*, *The Old North*.

Commemorating Gododdin warriors who were killed in battle against the Angles of Bernicia and Deira at Catraith in about 600 AD, the manuscript – known as *Llyfr Aneirin*, *Book of Aneirin* – is now in the precious care of Cardiff City Library.

Other important early works by Welsh poets include the fourteenth century *Red Book of Hergest*, now held in the Bodleian Library, Oxford, and the *White Book of Rhydderch*, kept in the National Library of Wales, Aberystwyth.

William Morgan's translation of the Bible into Welsh in 1588 is hailed as having played an important role in the advancement of the Welsh language, while in I885 Dan Isaac Davies founded the first Welsh language society.

It was in 1856 that Evan James and his son James James composed the rousing Welsh national anthem *Hen Wlad Fynhadad – Land of My Fathers*, while in the twentieth century the poet Dylan Thomas gained international fame and acclaim with poems such as *Under Milk Wood*.

The nation's proud cultural heritage is also celebrated through *Eisteddfod Genedlaethol Cymru*, the National Eisteddfod of Wales, the annual festival of music, literature and performance that is held across the nation and which traces its roots back to 1176 when Rhys ap Gruffyd, who ruled the territory of Deheubarth from 1155 to 1197, hosted a magnificent festival of poetry and song at his court in Cardigan.

The 2011 census for Wales unfortunately shows that the number of people able to speak the language has declined from 20.8% of the population of just under 3.1 million in 2001 to 19% – but overall the nation's proud culture, reflected in its surnames, still flourishes.

Many Welsh families proudly boast the heraldic device known as a Coat of Arms, as featured on our front cover.

The central motif of the Coat of Arms would originally have been what was borne on the shield of a warrior to distinguish himself from others on the battlefield.

Not featured on the Coat of Arms, but highlighted on page three, is the family motto and related crest – with the latter frequently different from the central motif.

Echoes of a far distant past can still be found in our surnames and they can be borne with pride in commemoration of our forebears.

Chapter two:

Invasion and conquest

A name with roots firmly embedded in the ancient soil of Wales, 'Bowen' is a patronymic form of the popular forename 'Owain' – derived from the Greek 'Eugenios', meaning 'noble', or 'well-born', and whose Anglicised form is 'Owen.'

Bearers of the Bowen name would have originally been known as, for example, Llewellyn ap Owain, or Llewellyn ab Owain, and in the case of the surname 'Bowen' it comes from a contraction of the 'ab' element prefixed to 'Owain', or 'Owen'.

In common with its counterpart in Ireland, the name has strong Celtic connections, but the two have completely different points of origin – with the Irish version stemming from 'Buadhacháin', meaning 'victorious.'

The Welsh form of the name, in the form of 'ap Oweyn', is recorded in 1292 in what is now the modern-day English county of Shropshire, while one historical source on the Bowens notes how one family of the name traces a descent from a Llewellyn ap Owen, recorded as having lived in the modern-day Welsh county of Pembrokeshire in 1364.

By 1424, the family are recorded as having adopted the 'Bowen' surname.

It is in Pembrokeshire, one of what are known as the thirteen historic Welsh counties, that the name is particularly identified.

This means that from earliest times the ancestors of those who would come to bear the name were at the centre of the high drama that is the nation's frequently turbulent history.

Known in the Welsh language as 'Sir Benfro', with 'Sir' indicating 'County', modern-day Pembrokeshire, in the southwest of Wales, has Haverfordwest as its county town, while previously it was Pembroke.

It is a rather unique county, in that in 1138, during the reign of England's King Stephen, it became divided between a predominantly Welsh speaking north and a mainly English speaking south.

So noticeable is this divide that the linguistic 'border' even has its own designation, known as the *Landsker Line* – derived from an old Anglo-Saxon term – while the south of the county is known as 'Little England in Wales.'

To unravel the highly genealogical skein of those 'Owains' or 'Owens' who would come to assume the Bowen surname, we have to travel back through the extremely dim mists of time to about 350 AD when an

Irish tribe, the Déisí, who were only a short voyage away from the southwest coastline of Wales, settled there.

It is in all likelihood because of their shared Celtic culture that they assimilated into the clanship of the Welsh tribes.

This cultural intermingling is thought to have led to the creation of the region known as Dyfed, and part of which later became the kingdom of Deheubarth.

It had been through the marriage of Hywel the Good, of the kingdom of Seisyllwg and who came to rule from Prestatyn to Pembroke between 915 AD and 950 AD, to Elen, heiress of Dyfed, that both kingdoms were united to form the kingdom of Deheubarth.

Approximately four centuries earlier, invaders had arrived in the form of the Anglo-Saxons – composed of the Jutes, from the area of the Jutland Peninsula in modern Denmark, the Saxons from Lower Saxony, in modern Germany and the Angles from the Angeln area of Germany.

Further invasion followed between approximately 950 AD and 1000, and the coastline of Wales was repeatedly subjected to raids by the Vikings who, when not raping and pillaging, established trading posts and settlements at Haverfordwest, Fishguard and Caldey Island.

But what was to eventually prove to be the

death knell of Welsh independence was sounded in the wake of the Norman Conquest of England in 1066.

A key date in not only English but also Welsh history, by 1066, England had become a nation with several powerful competitors to the throne.

In what were extremely complex family, political and military machinations, the English monarch was Harold II, who had succeeded to the throne following the death of Edward the Confessor.

But his right to the throne was contested by two powerful competitors – his brother-in-law King Harold Hardrada of Norway, in alliance with Tostig, Harold II's brother, and Duke William II of Normandy.

On October 14, Harold II encountered a mighty invasion force, led by Duke William that had landed at Hastings, in East Sussex.

Harold drew up a strong defensive position, at the top of Senlac Hill, building a shield wall to repel William's cavalry and infantry.

The Normans suffered heavy losses, but through a combination of the deadly skill of their archers and the ferocious determination of their cavalry they eventually won the day.

Anglo-Saxon morale had collapsed on the battlefield as word spread through the ranks that Harold, the last of the Anglo-Saxon kings, had been killed.

William was declared King of England on December 25, and the complete subjugation of his Anglo-Saxon subjects followed, with those Normans who had fought on his behalf rewarded with lands – a pattern that would be repeated in Wales.

Invading across the Welsh Marches, the borderland between England and Wales, the Normans gradually consolidated gains by building castles, for example, in what they called 'Penfro' – later to lend its name to the town of Pembroke.

Under a succession of Welsh leaders who included Llywelyn ap Gruffudd, known as Llywelyn the Last, resistance to what should now be more properly called the English yoke proved strong.

But it was brutally crushed in 1283 under England's ruthless and ambitious Edward I, who ordered the building or repair of at least 17 castles and in 1302 proclaiming his son and heir, the future Edward II, as Prince of Wales, a title known in Welsh as *Tywysog Cymru*.

Another heroic Welsh figure arose from 1400 to 1415 in the form of Owain Glyndŵr – the last native Welshman to be recognised by his supporters as *Tywysog Cymru*.

In what is known as The Welsh Revolt he achieved an early series of stunning victories against

Henry IV and his successor Henry V – until mysteriously disappearing from the historical record after mounting an ambush in Brecon.

Some sources assert that he was either killed in the ambush or died a short time afterwards from wounds he received – but there is a persistent tradition that he survived and lived thereafter in anonymity, protected by loyal followers.

During the revolt, he had consistently refused offers of a Royal Pardon and – despite offers of hefty rewards for his capture – he was never betrayed.

Meanwhile it was because of his popularity with his fellow native Welsh that many are thought to have adopted 'Owain' as a forename – later to develop into the Bowen surname.

Chapter three:

Honours and distinction

Noted for not only his legal acumen but also for his literary talent and wit, Charles Synge Christopher Bowen was the nineteenth century English judge elevated to the Peerage as Baron Bowen.

Born in 1835 in Woolaston, Gloucestershire, the son of a clergyman, and called to the bar in 1861, one of his famous cases as a prosecutor was that of 'The Tichborne Claimant' a lengthy case at the time that involved both a civil trial and a criminal trial.

It concerned a curious claim by Thomas Castro, also known as Arthur Orton, that he was the missing heir to the Tichborne Baronetcy in Hampshire.

The heir to the family title and fortune was Roger Tichborne, who was believed to have died in a shipwreck in 1854 while returning from South America.

But his grieving mother, having heard rumours that he was alive and living in Australia, placed advertisements in newspapers throughout the length and breadth of Australia offering a reward for any information on her son.

In 1866 a butcher known as Thomas Castro and who had been living in Wagga Wagga, New South Wales, came forward with the claim that he was actually Roger Tichborne.

Although Lady Tichborne accepted his claim, the rest of the family were highly sceptical and hired Bowen to represent their interests against the claimant in a civil court action.

Extensive inquiries into his background were undertaken and the case did not come to law until 1871 – with Bowen arguing skilfully against the claimant.

It then emerged that he might in fact be called Arthur Orton, a butcher's son from Wapping who had left home as a youth and had last been heard of in Australia.

His claim was dismissed and, charged with perjury, he was later brought before a criminal court. Found guilty, he was sentenced to 14 years imprisonment.

Later confessing that he was indeed Arthur Orton – only to immediately retract this – he died destitute in 1898.

Bowen's involvement in the case made him a household name, and he went on to hold high legal office as a judge on the Queen's Bench and was raised to the Peerage as Baron Bowen of Colwood, in the County of Essex.

A regular contributor to *The Spectator*, he is also credited with the phrase – to stress the need for complex legal matters to be expressed in a layperson's terms – "The man in the Clapham omnibus", while one of his quotations is:

The rain it raineth on the just
And also on the unjust fella,
But chiefly on the just, because
The unjust hath's the just's umbrella.

He died in 1894, while he was the brother of the Harrow School headmaster Edward Ernest Bowen; born in 1836, he died in 1901, having written the public school's song *Forty Years On*.

Travelling back in time to the eighteenth century, Emanuel Bowen was the English map engraver and geographer who carried out commissions for both George II and Louis XV of France.

Born in about 1694 and having established a business in London, he meticulously executed maps and engravings that include *Britannia Depicta*, published in 1720 and containing more than 200 road maps in addition to miniature maps of all the English and Welsh counties.

Despite his apparent success, he died in poverty in 1767, while he was the father of the maps and charts engraver Thomas Bowen.

His date of birth is not known, but it is known that he died in 1790 – in poverty, in common with his father – having published works that include his impressively entitled 1778 *A New And Accurate Map Of Europe From The Latest Improvements And Regulated By Astronomical Observations*.

A renowned geographer, particularly of his native Wales, Professor Emrys George Bowen, better known as E.G. Bowen, was born in Carmarthen in 1900, the son of an insurance agent.

The recipient in 1923 of a first-class honours degree in geography from University College of Wales, Aberystwyth, he was appointed a research fellow at the Welsh National School of Medicine, Cardiff, while also specialising in the nation's physical geography and social geography.

Appointed to the staff of the department of geography at University College of Wales, his many pioneering works include his 1954 *Settlements of the Celtic Saints of Wales*.

Also an assistant editor for a time with the *Encyclopaedia Britannica* and appointed president of the Institute of British Geographers in 1958, he died in 1983 – the recipient of other honours that included election as a Fellow of the Society of Antiquaries, while The E.G. Bowen Map Room at Aberystwyth University is named in his honour.

Bearers of the Bowen name have also excelled in the sciences.

Born in Worcester in 1898, Edmund ("Ted") John Bowen, better known as E.J. Bowen, was the English physical chemist noted for his research into the light phenomenon known as fluorescence and for which he received the prestigious Davy Medal in 1963.

Author of *The Chemical Aspects of Light* and carrying out his research work at the Trinity and Balliol College Laboratories in Oxford, he was present at a series of lectures delivered there in 1965 by Alfred Einstein.

He managed to obtain one of the blackboards used by Einstein to illustrate his lectures and presented it to the Museum of the History of Science, Oxford; he died in 1980.

Keeping a reputation for scientific excellence in the family, he was the father of the British chemist and botanist Humphry Bowen.

Born in Oxford in 1929, he specialised in research into radioisotopes and trace elements and the environmental effects of radiation.

Appointed a lecturer in chemistry at Reading University in 1964 and later as reader in analytical chemistry, it was as a consultant to the Dunlop Company that in 1967 he suggested the use of foam blocks to stem the oil from the Torrey Canyon oil disaster from spreading into the English Channel.

As a botanist and member of the Botanical

Society of the British Isles, he was the official recorder of plants for the English counties of Berkshire and Dorset while also a contributor of botanical data for *Flora of Oxfordshire*.

He died in 2001, while he was the father of the leading British computer scientist Jonathan P. Bowen.

Born in Oxford in 1956, posts he has held include professor of computer science at Birmingham City University and emeritus professor at London South Bank University.

One bearer of the proud name of Bowen who played a significant role in the achievement of Allied victory during the dark days of the Second World War was the Welsh physicist Edward George Bowen, also familiarly known as Taffy Bowen.

Born in 1911 at Cockett, Swansea, the son of a steelworker, he earned a first-class honours degree in physics and related subjects from Swansea University in 1930, and later completed postgraduate research on X-rays and the structure of alloys.

It was while working at the Radio Research Station, Slough, on a cathode-ray detection finder that he was 'head-hunted' by the scientist Robert Watson-Watt to join his team that was attempting to developed radar – derived from Radio Detection and Finding

The team successfully developed a system

whereby radio pulses were 'reflected' back from a target such as an aircraft, allowing for the early detection of incoming swarms of German Luftwaffe bombers and fighters – in turn enabling the 'scrambling' of fighter planes to meet and deal with the threat.

This played a crucial role not only during the Battle of Britain that was fought over the skies of southern and eastern England in the summer of 1940, but also in the detection of enemy submarines.

Appointed a year after the war ended to join the Commonwealth Scientific and Industrial Research Organisation (CSIRO), at its laboratories in Australia, Bowen was instrumental in promoting the science of radio astronomy and in the construction of the 201ft radio telescope at Parkes, New South Wales.

At the inauguration of the telescope in 1961, he stated: "The search for truth is one of the noblest aims of mankind and there is nothing which adds to the glory of the human race, or lends it such dignity, as the urge to bring the vast complexity of the Universe within the range of human understanding."

The Parkes Telescope, meanwhile, later proved invaluable to NASA for the success of its Apollo space missions while Bowen, the recipient of a CBE and a Fellow of the scientific think-tank the Royal Society, died in 1991.

Chapter four:
On the world stage

Best known for his role of Lieutenant Colonel Henry Blake in the 1975 film *M*A*S*H*, a wryly comedic look at the Korean War of 1950 to 1953, Roger Bowen was the American actor born in 1932 in Attleboro, Massachusetts.

One of the co-founders of the Chicago-based comedy and acting troupe The Second City, his other film credits include the 1968 *Petulia*, while television credits include, from 1970 to 1972, the sitcom *Arnie*; he died in 1996.

Known for her role from 2004 to 2012 of Julie Mayer in the television drama series *Desperate Housewives*, **Andrea Bowen** is the award-winning actress born in 1990 in Columbus, Ohio.

Of Welsh descent and making her stage debut at the tender age of six as Young Eponine in a Broadway production of *Les Misérables* – making her the youngest actor to ever play the role – her big screen credits include the 2013 *Scandal*.

The recipient in both 2011 and 2012 of a Primetime Emmy Award for Outstanding Actress for her role of Clare Dunphy in the American sitcom *Modern*

Family, Julie Bowen Luetkemeyer is the actress better known by her stage name of **Julie Bowen**.

Born in 1970 in Baltimore, Maryland, of English, Scottish, Irish, French and German descent, her big screen credits include the 1996 *Multiplicity*, the 2010 *Crazy on the Outside* and, from 2011, *Horrible Bosses*.

On British television screens, Peter Williams, born in 1937 in Wirral, Cheshire is the stand-up comedian and presenter better known as **Jim Bowen**.

A former deputy headmaster of a primary school near Lancaster, it was in the early 1960s that he first took to the stage as a stand-up comedian on the club circuit of northern England.

This led to television appearances on *The Wheeltappers and Shunters Social Club* and the 1975 to 1976 children's sketch show *You Must Be Joking*, but he is best known as having been the presenter of the ITV game show *Bullseye*.

The popular show involved general knowledge questions linked to skill in the game of darts, and Bowen became a household name with catchphrases that included – for unlucky contestants – "BHF", "Bus Fare Home."

With other television credits that include *Jonathan Creek* and *Phoenix Nights*, his solo show about

Bullseye – You Can't Beat a Bit of Bully – was performed at the Edinburgh Festival Fringe in 2005.

He died in 2018.

Born of Welsh descent in London in 1965, **Laurence Llewelyn-Bowen** is the television personality and home-style consultant who presented the series *Changing Rooms*.

Having founded his own design consultancy in 1989, he has also appeared as a judge on the reality show *Popstar to Opera Star* in addition to presenting the daytime show *Auction Party*.

On the frontline of international news, **Jeremy Bowen** is the award-winning Welsh journalist, foreign correspondent and television presenter born in Cardiff in 1960.

Having reported from war zones that include the Lebanon, the Balkans, Iraq and Syria, he is the recipient of awards that include a Sony Gold Award for News Story of the Year for his coverage of the apprehension and arrest in December of 2003 of former Iraqi leader Saddam Hussein.

Born in 1941 in Rangoon, India, the son of a British Army major general, Trevor Bowen is the screenwriter, actor and novelist better known as **T.R. Bowen**.

His television scriptwriting credits include the

1984 *Sherlock Holmes* series, *The Inspector Alleyn Mysteries*, *Lovejoy* and, from 2001, *Hornblower Mutiny*.

As an actor, he has had roles in television series that include the 1970 to 1972 *A Family at War* and *Judge John Deed*, while as a novelist his best-selling works include the 1971 *Punctuations*, the 1998 *The Death of Amy Parris* and, from 2002, *The Black Camel*.

Born in 1924, **John Griffith Bowen** is the British scriptwriter, playwright and novelist whose work for television includes the 1974 *The Treasure of Abbot Thomas* and the 1996 *Hetty Wainthrop: Woman of the Year*.

Bearers of the Bowen name have also excelled in the highly competitive world of sport – not least in the rough and tumble that is the game of rugby.

Born in 1895 in Morriston, **Cliff Bowen** was the Welsh player who earned three caps playing for his nation; also an accomplished cricket player, at one stage representing Carmarthenshire, he died in 1929.

Born in Swansea in 1863, **George Bowen** was the Welsh rugby union half-back who, in addition to playing for Swansea and Llanelli, also earned four caps playing for his nation.

He died in 1919, while Benjamin John Bowen, better known as **Jackie Bowen**, was the international rugby league player born in Llanelli; playing for a period with Wigan and having served during the Second World War with the Welsh Guards, he died in 2009.

Capped thirteen times for Wales, **William Bowen** was the rugby union player born in 1862 in the original Bowen heartland of Pembrokeshire; having played club rugby for Swansea, he died in 1925.

From the rugby pitch to the fields of European football, **Mark Bowen** is the Welsh former left-back who, in addition to playing at international level, also played for clubs that include Tottenham Hotspur, Norwich City, West Ham United and Reading.

Born in 1963 in Neath, since retiring as a player in 1999 he has worked as an assistant manager for the Welsh international team and for clubs that include Manchester City, Fulham, Queens Park Rangers and Stoke City.

The recipient of nineteen caps for Wales, David Lloyd Bowen, better known as **Dave Bowen**, was the player who captained his team in what is, to date, his nation's only World Cup finals.

This was in 1958 when, having qualified for the quarter-finals, they were knocked out after being beaten 1-0 by Brazil – the goal being scored by a 17-year-old Pelé.

Born in 1928 in Maesteg, Bowen played for clubs that include Arsenal and Northampton Town – managing the latter for eight years.

He died in 1995, while the North Stand of Northampton's Sixfield Stadium is named in his honour.

Bearers of the Bowen name have also stamped their mark on the creative worlds of music and literature.

Born in 1937, **Jimmy Bowen** is the American record producer and former solo pop star whose first hit was the 1957 *I'm Stickin' With You*, which earned him a gold disc.

As a record producer, he has worked with artists ranging from Nancy Sinatra and Lee Hazelwood to Frank Sinatra, Glen Campbell, Kenny Rogers and Garth Brookes, while as a composer of movie soundtracks his credits include the 1970 *Vanishing Point*, the 1980 *Smokey and the Bandit II* and the 1985 *Slugger's Wife*.

In the world of literature, **Elizabeth Bowen** was the Anglo-Irish novelist and short story writer born in Dublin in 1899.

As a writer she mixed with what was known as the Bloomsbury Group, and her early novels include the 1929 *The Last September* and, from 1938, *Death of the Heart*.

Leading a rather unconventional lifestyle, she was married to the teacher and later BBC executive Alan

Cameron – but the marriage was never consummated and she had a string of affairs.

Working for the British Ministry of Information during the Second World War and, drawing on her experiences in wartime London, she wrote other acclaimed works that include *Eva Trout* and *The Demon Lover and Other Stories*.

The recipient of a CBE for her services to literature, she died in 1973.

A noted American biographer, **Catherine Drinker Bowen** was born in 1897 in Haverford, Pennsylvania.

Winner in 1958 of the U.S. National Book Award for Nonfiction for *The Lion and the Throne: The Life and Times of Sir Edward Coke* and the recipient in 1962 of the Women's National Book Association Award, she died in 1973.

One particularly heart warning tale concerning bearers of the proud name of Bowen relates to the busker and internationally best-selling author **James Bowen** and his faithful feline friend Bob.

Born in Surrey in 1979 and moving to Australia with his mother after his parents divorced, his early life was beset with problems.

Not managing to settle into the family home or at school, he describes himself at the time as having been "a tearaway kid", and was diagnosed as suffering from schizophrenia, manic depression and ADHD (Attention Deficit Hyperactivity Disorder).

Moving back to Britain when he was aged 19, his life spiralled out of control as he became addicted to heroin and began sleeping rough in London.

Weaning himself off heroin by entering a methadone programme, he began busking and was befriended in 2007 by a stray ginger cat that he named Bob.

The pair soon became a tourist attraction as James, always accompanied by Bob, busked in Covent Garden and in Piccadilly – and it was through Bob that he was able to wean himself off the methadone programme.

With tourists posting videos of the pair to YouTube, they came to the attention of publishers Hodder and Stoughton, who teamed James up with the author Garry Jenkins.

The result has been *A Street Cat Named Bob*, first published in March of 2012, and followed by other best-sellers that include *The World According to Bob* and *A Gift from Bob*.

Meanwhile *A Street Cat Named Bob*, which has been published in more than 30 languages, has sold more than one million copies alone in the UK.